KNIT

KNIT

*Discover that you have ALWAYS been knit
for Every challenge and Every success*

ANTOINETTE STEWART

Ms. A,
The work you do is of tremendous importance. May you continue to embody the Christ like character of "Teachin" as you impact and influence the next generation! Thank you,
Tom

KNIT

To my children, whom I admire and love, leave your own legacy.

KNIT

CONTENTS

Introduction

One: In Utero

Two: Breathe

Three: The Problem with Pain

Four: Dilating Decisions

Five: The Demanded Gift

Six: Let's Name it Grace

CONCLUSION

KNIT

Foreword

By # 1 Best Selling Author Pastor Levi Harrell

Upon research, I found out that the name Antoinette means "High Praise." Which I find to be very appropriate for someone who walks with great integrity.

When I think of Antoinette Stewart, I immediately think of terms such as precision, accuracy, excellence, and focus. A woman of great faith and great determination. I think of someone who gained the ability to defy all the odds that life stacked against her only to rise from the ashes with great wisdom, courage, and strength. I believe it is this Wisdom that you will see gracefully throughout the pages of this eye-opening book.

When I first heard of the title of the book; "Knit." My mind automatically thought about the knitting process. The process of knitting is one wherein a series of loops or knots are woven together or interlinked to create one undivided thread. As you continue doing this it ultimately creates a larger form of material that can be designed for a blanket, scarf, hat, socks, or more. This is an interesting

KNIT

concept to me because just like life. We all go through a series of ups, downs, hurts, heartbreaks, good days and bad days...for the sake of this moment, we will call this the "Knots of Life."

It's these knots of life that interlink in the process of knitting that creates the masterpiece that we all are today. Every pain, every tear, and every sleepless night is only a knot being woven together to work out for our good.

I believe Romans 8:28 says it best, "And we know that all things work together for good to those who love God, to those who are the called according to His purpose."

In other words, if you're called and loved by God there is no such thing as aimless occurrences. Nothing just happens...everything serves a purpose and whether it feels like it or not, please understand that it's all working in your favor.

As you read this work of literature, I want you to fully grasp the heart of what Apostle-Elect Stewart has written and fully engage in the knitting process.

KNIT

In Fact, enjoy the process and know that God has you in mind. He knows all. He sees all and He has specifically handcrafted you knot by knot and loop by loop.

- Pastor Levi W. Harrell

KNIT

Introduction

Psalm 139:13

For you created my inmost being you knit me together in my mother's womb.

I've always admired people who could sit for hours at a time knitting, weaving yarn or wool in and out to produce a garment of some sort. This is a skill that I have never possessed. The likely hood of the end product mirroring what I imagined is highly unlikely.

I just don't have the patience to knit. I would want to complete the blanket, sweater, or baby bootie, as quickly as possible, because the carefulness of each detail would drive me crazy.

If measuring to ensure it fits an actual person or pet is involved then you can forget it, that is *definitely* not my calling!

It always amazes me how knitters have great attention to detail and can produce a design or pattern free handed. Each woven motion is

KNIT

intentional and carefully guided. In comparison to David, the psalmist would carefully use the word knit to describe how the Creator, God. has created His children.

To knit or to be knitted is to be united or caused to unite. To be knitted means to cause a thing or things to stride together, to be brought together and to be made by interlocking.

Think about it, God, the creator, our Father, has knitted us together. If you are like me, you thought that He just attached our arms to our shoulders, our head to our neck, legs to our hips, etc. Right?

Well yes and no. He indeed put every body part in its rightful place, but that isn't the end of the knitting. He knit together our entire lives and everything we would need to enter life. He caused it to unite. Even the things that we think don't fit.

He causes the disappointment to stride together with our purpose. He causes the setback to be brought together with ambition. Failure to be interlocked with determination to produce drive and motivation. He knitted it all together to work out for our good (Romans 8:28)!

The knitting did not stop at our biology, psychology, or anatomy but it is extended to stride together with our destiny! As we explore the beautiful patterns of our lives being woven together,

KNIT

even the dingy, dirty, shrunken pieces, let us remember that we are "knit for this!"

Father, thank you that I am fearfully and wonderfully made in the brilliant image of Your son Jesus Christ. Wash over me Father as I open my heart and mind to Your spirit. Please allow me to understand Your thoughts although they are not my thoughts neither are my ways your ways. As the heavens are higher than the earth, so are Your ways higher than my ways and your thoughts than my thoughts. Therefore, I rely on You Father to show me the way and give me victorious thoughts, thoughts that I could never give myself. Father, You knit me for Your glory. Please help me to remain intact and in sync with Your design for my life. Thank You Majesty. In Jesus name I pray, Amen.

one

In Utero

Psalm 139:16

Thine eyes did see my substance yet being unperfect; and in thy book all my members were written, which in continuance were fashioned, when as yet there was none of them.

Let me start off by saying that God did not give humans the *spirit* of a coward (2 Timothy 1:7). When fear is present ask yourself what is on the other side of this fear? What is being kept from me by this barrier or fortress of fear?

I personally do not like being afraid. If I am faced with an obstacle of fear my natural reaction is to confront the obstacle, remove it, and move past the presence of fear.

Some of life's toughest decisions hold a great weight of uncertainty and fear. Who do I marry?

KNIT

Where do I live? Where do I work? Should I have children? These are just a few of the major decisions we will face in this lifetime.

If we would be honest, many of the decisions we've made, if given the chance, we would alter or modify that decision in some way or another. Maybe even get rid of it all together and start over. I believe that is why God made it impossible to turn back the hands of time.

I love time traveling movies such as <u>Back to the Future</u> and <u>Bill and Ted's Excellent Adventure</u>. I know, I just dated myself, don't judge me.

What I love about these movies is that almost always those who desire to travel back to the past are warned "do not change anything." One small change could alter something as serious as a child never being born.

Before I answered the call to ministry God challenged me to put all that I've learned through church going, Bible studies, and faith filled experiences into practice.

The very first ministry context that I was led to was a center for pregnancy help. I had driven pass this facility dozens of times on my route to and from home. One day the Holy Spirit told me to stop and inquire about becoming a volunteer.

I had no idea what took place inside of the center. I assumed it was a place where mothers who were experiencing the possibility or reality of an unplanned pregnancy could go for resources, *options*, and help.

My assumptions were somewhat true. The center indeed was a place where suspected and expected pregnancies were the priority, but it was also rich soil for ministry! I was pleasantly surprised when the volunteer application presented questions about my relationship with Jesus and my salvation and conversion experience.

Prior to my application being approved I visualized that some of my duties would be answering the telephone, making appointments, stocking supplies, etc. Oh, was I wrong! My assignment in the center was to provide godly counsel to the clients. Who would've thought? God, of course!

The significance of God assigning me to this ministry is that I knew unplanned pregnancy all too well. As a matter of fact, most of the young ladies who walked into the center contemplating abortion walked out confident that they could make a *decision* to choose life. They were able to see the product of an unplanned pregnancy standing before them. Me.

I was not the result of some well thought out parental plan and maybe you weren't either. I don't know how your conception came about, but the way I came into the earth was much less than planned.

KNIT

My mother became pregnant with me at the age of 14 and admittedly so she found herself feeling like many of the expected mothers who walked into the center for pregnancy help, she had options, a decision to make, and she chose life.

It may seem as though the blessing of my testimony was strictly for the clients that I served but that would be the furthest thing from the truth. The blessing in the testimony was for me.

During my experience ministering to scared mothers to be, I too came to realize that God in all His wisdom *knit* me! He chose the perfect womb of a 14-year-old girl to craft me and carry me into the realm of time.

I spent most of my adult life up to that point not realizing how much power was locked into an impossible situation. I want to encourage you that there is power in your seemingly impossible situation too! He *knit* you for the challenge. He *knit* you to come through.

My embarrassing beginning would give people (unborn children) whom I will probably never meet a chance to be given life. WOW, you mean to tell me that my parents failure to plan worked together to accomplish God's much bigger plan?

One of the toughest truths to wrap our minds around is that there was indeed an interaction that took place between God and ourselves before we ever

KNIT

took a breath. This is what He said to the prophet Jeremiah, "I *knew you* before I formed you in your mother's womb."

Surely Jeremiah was not the only person God knew before they were born! He knew you too! He knew you in and before utero.

According to the Strong's Concordance the word knew in the Greek is ginóskó which means to come to know, recognize, perceive. This type of knew is the result of personal and experiential knowledge of a person.

If we put the word knew according to Jeremiah 1:5 into context we might conclude that God had a personal relationship and an experience with Jeremiah that was obtained by personal commitment.

The same goes for all of us. God has a personal commitment to His believers. He had an experience with us before the red lines appeared on the plastic test strip, before the nurse confirmed that our mothers were indeed pregnant, before mom ever missed her monthly cycle, God had a personal commitment to YOU. Therefore, we have this confidence that although we cannot remember or even fathom this foreknowing encounter, the encounter indeed took place.

Let's look at our introductory scripture to gain a clearer understanding of this truth. David, the king,

KNIT

affirms that he was confident that God covered him, which could be translated that God "wove him together" in utero.

David used the word "substance" which for this context, in Hebrew, indicates that he was describing an embryo. David expresses that in his unformed state, God had already fashioned all his days for him and recorded these days in His book.

Meaning, all of our yesterdays, today's, and tomorrows have already been dressed up and placed in God's memorabilia. What does this mean for you and me?

The solid truth is this, your decisions, be it right or wrong in *your* sight, does not somehow cause you to have more power to destroy your life than God has power to redeem your life.

This means that we can focus less on the outcome and more on the income or in another word, gains. We can focus less on what we've lost, what went wrong, who wronged us, and the step we missed. We can redirect our attention to all that we have gained and will gain as our story of redemption unfolds with each breath that we take. Now, RELAX, and breathe.

Father, I am called by Your name, I humble myself before you, and pray, and seek Your face, and turn from my wicked ways. Father, You are faithful even when I am not. Even in my limited understanding

KNIT

You continue to shield me in the covenant of a greater promise. Father, I surrender all my fibers to You. I am confident that I can trust Your orchestration of love, promise, and patience with me. Thank You King, in Jesus name I pray. Amen.

KNIT

-Reflect-

two

Breathe

Job 12:10 (KJV)

In whose hand is the soul of every living thing, and the breath (ruach) of all mankind.

One thing that used to baffle me is how it was possible for a baby to breathe while floating in amniotic fluid, the liquid that surrounds the baby in the womb (uterus), but impossible for humans to breathe under water?

I could not understand God's plan for not allowing humans to breathe under water. I asked Him why did He created us this way? And He answered, kind of. One thing that I absolutely love about being a student of the Word is that He does not just give us the answer. He doesn't fish for you He teaches you to fish for yourself. Therefore, I went fishing for the answer.

I had no idea that one little piece of bait would snag such a big fish! This is what I discovered as I fished

KNIT

for an answer to the fore mentioned question. Babies don't truly breathe in the womb!

Instead, the umbilical cord provides the baby with oxygen until it takes its first breath.

While in utero the baby is absorbing the liquid, and it looks like the fetus is breathing but he/she is actually swallowing.

The umbilical cord is the source of oxygen and according to Medical News Today, if the umbilical cord remains intact, there should be no risk of drowning in or outside the womb.

I have a few questions for you, I know, I ask a lot of questions. But seriously, are you breathing? Or do you *look* like you are breathing? Are you going through the motions, but in reality are you taking a lot in, but not letting anything out?

The wretched reality is this, most people have a *breathing motion,* but are not breathing. They have a smile on their face but hurting inside-breathing *motion*. They are dressed well, smell good, but they suffer with insecurity- breathing *motion*. They are the life of the party, but they go home to an empty house of loneliness- breathing *motion*. These people go to church every Sunday yet remain powerless- breathing *motion*. They go to work every day yet feeling unfulfilled and purposeless- breathing *motion*. I think you get the point. It is very possible to be suffocating and perpetrating as if you are

KNIT

living, but in actuality you are only existing and tolerating each day and all that it brings.

It is time for you to stop going through the motions and actually breathe! Most often we get stuck on the wheel of motion because we anticipate failure and disappointment. We are too afraid to just breath!

We see what we want yet we increase the distance between *it* and ourselves by being convinced by our own expected end. But guess what? God has an expected end also!

Jeremiah 29:11 (my remix) "For I **know** the thoughts that I have..." this means God doesn't need *you* to know, He got this. But if you must know, then here it is, "the thoughts I thinks toward you are thoughts of peace, and not of evil, to give you an *expected end."*

This is a strong indication that we should learn to make our expectations line up with God's expectations!

Once we form our expectations based on the promises of God, we then learn that it is now His responsibility to do what He said He would do.

Our stance is trust, our position is hunkered down in faith, and our ability to execute is in our reliability on every Word that precedes out of His mouth.

I am convinced that we are responsible for the stewardship of everything that God has given us,

KNIT

even the very breath that we breath. Essentially, it still belongs to Him. It is still in His hand (Job 12:10).

I am reminded of the parable of the talents in Matthew 25:14 30 as I think about stewarding the breath that God has given us.

What will you return to God as it pertains to the breath He has given you? Will you have anything to show for all the risings and fallings of your chest cavity? Will you tell Him that you were too afraid to relax and breath because you feared failing? Or maybe you will tell Him that you were "saving your breath" when He told you to declare His truth in the earth.

Oh! I know what you will tell Him. You will tell Him that you are a realist and you do not have time to allow experiences that may *take your breath away* or better yet, you are to insecure to believe that a *breath taking* amazing experience could actually happen to you. You held on to your breath, never letting anyone or anything "take it away."

You live safely under the umbrella of logic and sense. Ideas like *true love* and *abundant living* are just concepts conceived by fantasy and *you,* of course, do not have time to live in a fantasy world.

You my dear, you are absolutely worthy of *breath-taking* experiences! Matter of fact, God's blessings for you are already yours, they were preordained!

KNIT

He has a plethora of breath-taking experiences for you!

Even better, He promises that His blessings will make you rich and He will add no sorrow with them (Proverbs 10:22). Try that on for size! I guarantee that it will fit you well.

If I have not already described the type of person you are then maybe, you are the type who believe that saying "I'm sorry" or "I forgive you" is a *waste of breath.* The absence of forgiveness can cause a severed relationship. A relationship that is fueled by the fear of rejection and dysfunctional perception makes one think that they are *losing,* or that the other person has won. Can I tell you a secret? In reconciliation and forgiveness, everyone wins.

Reconciliation protects reputation. Reconciliation also puts believers in the position to demonstrate God's love and power in the earth. Through Christ we are reconciled to the Father, with Christ it is possible to be reconciled to one another.

You were pre-wired/knit to administer the ministry of reconciliation, it is how you are being conformed to the image of His Son, Jesus Christ (Romans 8:29-30).

Perhaps, you are the "I won't hold my breath" type of person. This person has been disappointed by God. They still acknowledge that He is God and that He exists, but they refuse to get their hopes up

KNIT

and believe that God would give them what they desire.

The "I won't hold my breath" person will not take risks. They've been scarred by the *wait* seasons of their life. Their attitude is "if you do it God then good, if You don't, that's cool too. Either way I am safe from disappointment."

If this is you, the truth that God has already written your story is so farfetched to you. To be quite honest, the truth that He knew about every disappointment that you would face may actually cause more disappointed for you, especially if you are not able to see how God is sovereign and nothing is wasted in Him. I have a special place in my heart for people who are disappointed and frustrated with God. I have been there.

In 2017 my husband abandoned my children and me. To say that I was devastated is an understatement. I could not believe that God would actually allow this to happen to my family. During that season of my life I could not fathom how the abandonment would somehow work out for the good of me and my children. But it did! The abandonment caused me to utilize strength and courage that I never knew that I had. And out of the abandonment was the courage to write the book you are reading.

If I may encourage you:

KNIT

It has not yet entered your heart the things that God has in store for you. Every good and perfect gift. Even disappointment offers us gifts such as growth, resiliency, and wisdom.

Gifts that we may have never received had it not been for a disappointment or two...or three...ok, or more. But if you would stay in faith God's plan will surely unfold.

Be encouraged in this, God the Father is omniscient and knows just how many breaths He has given to each of His children. He manages them very well. They too, breaths, were a subject matter as He planned the air quality needed for your destination travel here on earth!

Ezekiel was challenged in chapter thirty-seven the ninth verse to "Prophesy to the breath; prophesy, son of man, and say to it, 'This is what the Sovereign LORD says: Come, breath, from the four winds and breathe into these slain, that they may live."

I challenge YOU to prophesy to your breath!

Tell it to breathe into and revive every dream that has been smothered by the pressure of mediocrity. Prophesy that your breath will not be wasted on activity that keep you from advancing in your God given, predestined, purposed here on earth.

Give your breath an assignment, tell it to breathe on the flickering ember of your zeal for the things of

KNIT

the Kingdom of God, your desire to live boldly and ignite a fire for God.

I prophesy to YOUR breath that it will no longer be breathing to death, but it will LIVE and give life! Your breath will breathe life into a people, hopes, dreams, visions, businesses, ministries, and even situations!

Father breathe new life in me. I need a revival on the inside of me. Father allow me to live afresh and new discovering new possibilities and experience new faith. End the gasping for air moments in my life that keep me in a suffocated space where I can't run freely for You. Release me from chambers of toxicity, doubt and denial. Father, increase my spiritual stamina, set my pace, and supply me fresh air for the distance. Father, Your surpassing goodness takes my breath away. I love You Majesty, in Jesus name I pray. Amen.

KNIT

-Reflect-

KNIT

three

The Problem with Pain

John 9:3

Jesus answered. "This happened so the power of God could be seen in him."

The problem with pain is that children of God find it hard to comprehend that God would allow and even go so far as to use pain to carry out His plan for our lives. But Jesus.

The painful reality of Jesus' life on earth is proof that pain is pregnant with purpose and delivers God's promises.

The irony is that we are promised pain in John 16:33, but somehow we think that pain is deliberately contrary to what we expect. We are often amused by the realization that pain is necessary.

Imagine this scene from a good action movie.

KNIT

Bad guys force their way into the home of a well-known wealthy investor. They knock the investor out with a blow to the back of the head, throw a bag over the investors face, kidnap the investor and take him to an undisclosed location.

When the investor awakes, he is tied to a chair in the middle of a dusty warehouse surrounded by angry looking bad guys.

Immediately upon the investors alertness the bad guys begin to interrogate him asking him questions such as "where is the money?" The investor still trying to keep his dignity and respect boldly refused to give an answer.

After several attempts trying to get the investor to reveal the location of the money; the bad guys are still unsuccessful. The bad guys now begin to physically harm the investor.

Initially, the investor remains tough taking every blow like a champ.

The bad guys grow extremely angry and less patient with the investor. They hit him with a blow that causes excruciating pain, and before we know it the investor is screaming out the response they have been demanding all along.

Pain demands a response. It is very rare that a person such as youself and I can experience pain give absolutely no response to the pain.

KNIT

Have you ever stubbed your toe in the middle of the night? You probably wanted to scream a combination of colorful words out loud, but you couldn't because your entire house is sleeping. You responded by grabbing your foot and hopping foolishly to the bathroom, the kitchen or wherever your middle of the night destination may have been.

Emotional, spiritual, and mental pain are no different. There are many responses to these types of pain depending on the severity of the pain. Some blows are less harmful causing a slight response. But then, there are those blows that knock the wind right out of us and drop us to our knees. The big blows are typically the ones that cause us to question God's sovereignty, His plan, His love for us and even in some cases His deity.

A few years ago, I was hit by a devastating blow. My experience was much like the movie scene I described earlier. Initially, I was unbothered and certain that God was going to show up and make it all better. Well, He didn't. The situation did not change, in fact it got much worst. The worse it grew the more intolerable the pain. I admit my response was horrible. I had several responses and most of them were shameful. But there was one. One response that made it all make sense, that response was to surrender to His will.

During my experience with pain, I had a very hard time wrapping my head around the purpose of the

KNIT

pain I was experiencing. I had a lot of questions. I asked God, "what is the purpose of pain for a believer?" I mean, we already believe, we are already saved, why do we need pain?

I discovered that the purpose of pain for a believer is twofold, one, we are predestined to be conformed to the image of His son (Romans 8:29). Pain somehow humbles us, and we become more like Christ in our humility.

Pain has a way of detoxing us from those things that cause us to look *much less* than the image of Christ. Since we are predestined to be conformed, in some cases, pain causes the rapid response and rapid release of that conformity.

Two, pain causes a response from the Father of compassion, the God of all comfort who comforts us so that we can comfort others when they are in trouble/pain (2 Corinthians 1:4).

Pain keeps God's never-ending circle of comfort and love rotating through mankind; thus causing strength and unity in the Body and confidence in the faith that we profess.

Here is where relief happened for me. I hope this will help you in your process as well, Ephesians 1:11 says this, Furthermore, because we are united (knit) with Christ, we have received an inheritance from God, for He chose us in advance, and he makes everything work out according to his plan.

KNIT

Every tear, every sleepless night, every lost appetite He chose in advance to work it all out according to His plan. In advance. The King James version says it like this "being predestinated according to the purpose of him who worketh all things after the counsel of his own will" That is powerful!

God's will provides counsel to our situations. In other words, it tells our pain what to do and its role in His will!

Everything must submit to the counsel of God's will; the authoritative, final decision-making counsel, of His will. Why? Because we were/are predestined. Whatever hits us will knock us in the direction of God's providence and plan.

Check this out, James says something crazy to us in chapter 1. What he instructs us to do would convince most of us that maybe he has lost his mind or perhaps he hasn't been through anything that has truly tested his faith.

James had the nerve, the audacity to tell us to consider it *pure joy* when all hell has broken loose in our lives. Maybe not in those exact words, but to make it plain.

James instructs us to consider hard times an opportunity for joy.

Now, I don't know about you, but if I were seeking an opportunity for *joy* it certainly wouldn't be in the trials and tribulations of life. An opportunity for joy

KNIT

sounds more like a vacation to Dubai or Tahiti. But joy in *pain*, not at all!

BUT! James was sharing pure wisdom. He says, "Consider it pure joy, my brothers and sisters, whenever you face trials of many kinds, because you know that the testing of your faith produces perseverance. Let perseverance <u>finish its work</u> so that you may be mature and <u>complete</u>, not lacking anything."

God hired perseverance! He gave perseverance a job to do, a work to finish in YOU! When did He do that? Yup, you guessed correctly, before you were even *knit* in your mother's womb. It has always been God's will for you to lack nothing and one of the employees He uses to ensure that there is no lack is perseverance.

Listen, some situations in life are beyond painful. I would never try to make light of anyone's pain. Each person experiences their painful situation differently and their pain is more real to them than it is to anyone else.

Maybe you are amid a painful experience at this moment of your life and the last thing on your mind is joy or perseverance. Allow me to offer you a bit of encouragement. I would like for you to know that God sees you and each day, whether you realize it or not, perseverance is working on your behalf.

KNIT

You may feel defeated, like this situation is wearying you out, but the truth is found in Daniel 7:25-28, it champions us to believe that although the enemy tries to wear out the saints, "...all his power will be taken away and completely destroyed."

The blood of Jesus is a mighty warrior! It will never lose its power, authority, or dominion. Just as promised in Exodus 12:13 The blood will be a sign for you and when God sees the blood, no affliction shall happen to you *to* destroy you. The weapon of affliction may form but it will not destroy you!

I love what 2 Corinthians 4:9 says at the very end of the verse after it tells us that we may be hard pressed on every side, but not crushed.

Paul continues by saying that we may be perplexed, but not in despair; persecuted, but not abandoned; and even struck down, but after all of that Paul tells us the answer that we all need to hear, "but not destroyed."

This pain will not destroy you. Even *it* must fall under subjection to God's predestined plan for your life!

Father, thank You for being faithful to wipe away every tear and collecting them, keeping them secure in Your presence where they are not forgotten nor miscounted or disregarded. Father, please remind me that even pain has potential that cannot escape

KNIT

Your grasping and gripping love for me. Father, thank you that pain can be a catalyst to purpose and a proponent to my growth in the faith. Let my response be pleasing in Your sight. In Jesus name I pray. Amen.

KNIT

-Reflect-

KNIT

four

Dilating Decisions

Ephesians 1:3-4

All praise to God, the Father of our Lord Jesus Christ, who has blessed us with every spiritual blessing in the heavenly realms because we are united with Christ. Even before he made the world, God loved us and chose us in Christ to be holy and without fault in his eyes.

What if I told you that everything that we consider the future is already the past to God? That our lives are a beautiful love story set on replay for an audience of One, the Director, Editor, Screenwriter, and Producer Himself, God?

KNIT

Well it is true, everything that is to come He has already seen, and He is patiently watching this love thriller-drama play out and YOU are the Star!

Everything that you are and will become, you have always been! You and your life are a product of design. Your look, functions and workings, all prepackaged! When I discovered this truth, my life took on new meaning, my perspective changed, and my confidence in God's ability to not lose sight of me in the haystack grew immensely.

I have another question for you. What if I proposed that one of the most feared things that people suffer with is the one thing that statisticians all over the globe fail to equate in their data collection. It is amongst the very top fears that human beings face in their lifetime?

If you use your internet search engine to query top fears that humans face, this fear that I am about to introduce to you will rarely show up in the lofty list of fears. When in fact it should be listed right up there next to death and public speaking.

I bet you are thinking, "What is it already?" I am glad you asked (smirk). This hiding in plain sight fear is called decidophobia. It is a fancy word that means the fear of making the wrong decisions.

Decidophobia is a term coined by Princeton University philosopher Walter Kaufmann in his book <u>Without Guilt and Justice</u>.

KNIT

Most humans spend more time contemplating and dilating a decision than making the decision. Why is this? The reason behind our continual contemplation and in some cases, procrastination, is the perceived consequence or fear of failure.

The word dilate means to make or become wider, larger, or more open. According to the Strong's Concordance the Greek word for wide is platus translated "broad" or "a street".

This chapter is strategically named Dilating Decisions to point you to this concept, the decisions that we make, open or make wider opportunities and relationships.

A decision that you have made may have been a seemingly bad decision, but I am almost certain that decision caused you to encounter people or opportunities that you may have never encountered had you neglected to make the decision.

Proverbs 16:9 tells us this, a man's heart plans his way, But the LORD directs his steps. We make plans and God decides how those plans will be carried out; again, knitting together the facets of our lives, showing His total involvement in the lives of His creation.

As a reformed decidophobic (I just made that up), meaning a person who feared making the wrong decision. I found it extremely liberating when I discovered the truth of God's word about life, my

KNIT

life, your life and God's ever reaching hand in our missteps, milestones and moments, all of them.

One of my favorite stories and characters in the Bible is Jonah. I love that guy. He is such a timeless character. I have heard the story of Jonah preached several times, and yet it still never gets old to me.

Here you have a guy who was given an assignment by God that he did not want. Some scholars have named Jonah an anti-missionary who rejected God's call. I personally think they are too hard on the guy. I mean really, God can come up with some pretty interesting assignments if you ask me.

Jonah heard the word of the Lord that told him to go to Nineveh and cry out against that city because of their wickedness. Jonah's response was to run away from the assignment and from the presence of God. Most of us know the story so I will not transcribe it here. The things that stood out most to me about Jonah's story are:

1. Jonah thought that He could escape God's presence. He thought God's presence was geographical. (1:3)
2. In his disobedience Jonah made a decision that not only negatively affected himself but almost got others killed. (1:4)
3. Jonah did not lose his identity during his disobedience. (1:9)
4. Jonah took responsibility for his decision and tried to make it right. (1:12)

5. The Lord was prepared for Jonah's escape attempt. (1:17)
6. Jonah came to a place of repentance and remembered the Lord. (2:1-10)
7. Jonah ended up right where he should've been in the first place. (3:3)
8. Jonah expressed genuine emotion toward God about God's plan and outcome of the situation. (4:1-9)

What grips my heart in Jonah's story the most are points 8 and 9. Jonah had a relationship with God that allowed him to be a total person. He did not hide the side of himself that most of us hide…his anger, his depression, his dissatisfaction about an outcome that God allowed. When God asked him questions, he was honest with God. And the most interesting thing is that he did what God told him to do while battling and wrestling with these emotions.

The fact that God allowed him to detour YET had a prepared strategy to route him back to his assignment shows us that no matter how crazy the decision, we cannot escape God's plan. Notice in chapter one verse sixteen it describes the sailors having reverential fear, piety and believing faith and even offering their sacrifices to the God of Israel. What appeared to be what would kill them brought them salvation!

Maybe you are struggling with an act of disobedience or a decision you've made and you

KNIT

feel that you have really messed up; even put others in harm's way. Please be encouraged, God is still the God of salvation and can save us all the way up until the end! His word declares that even if you make your bed in hell, He will be with you. I love that Jesus took the keys to hell and death. This means that there is no limit to where He can grab us and rescue us from.

I pray that you are liberated, encouraged, and filled with immeasurable confidence as we unlock and discover the truth about God's involvement in our existence, His infinitely intelligent planning, and His nonnegotiable wisdom.

Now, I need you to make a decision, pun intended, decide to abandon your fear of decision making. Making *no* decision limits you, deciding opens (dilates) you to brand new opportunities.

Father, in the name of Jesus I declare that every seemingly bad decision is working together for my good. Everything that the devil meant for evil You O' Lord are working it for my good. Father, I believe in Your forgiveness and that I can be a total person before You. You created my inner most parts and there is nothing about me that You do not know. I do not have the power to overthrow Your Kingdom that lives in me. You designed me and my life since before the beginning of time and nothing and no one can change Your mind to love me. In Jesus name I pray. Amen.

KNIT

-Reflect-

five
The Demanded Gift

Proverbs 18:16

A man's gift maketh room for him, and bringeth him before great men.

My children and I were preparing for an unplanned transition in our lives. The transition included moving across the country from the state of Washington to South Carolina. My son, who was 16 years old at the time was in total disagreement with the move. For good reason of course. He was being ripped away from his friends and what had become a normal life for him.

One morning as we were packing and preparing for our move we sat on boxes in a nearly empty room in our home and had a very colorful discussion about his feelings about the move. He expressed how he felt. He expressed that he felt like he had more opportunities to be successful in his athletics and musical giftings where we were in Washington.

KNIT

As a mother, I heard all sorts of emotions in my child's plea to stay where we were, to not shake things up, to keep things safe and secure. Unfortunately, the move had to happen, and it had to happen now. As he expressed his concerns, I frantically searched my wisdom for the right answer to comfort and assure him that things were going to work out just fine, but the answer was not in my wisdom, it was in the Word of God.

In this moment Proverbs 18:16 took on a brand-new meaning. In this moment of conversation with my extremely talented and gifted son, the Holy Spirit stepped in and rescued me from being the "because I said so" mom and provided sweet revelation.

The Word revealed that the gifts given to us by Abba Father are relentless. They are demanding and demanded! The dialogue between my son and I shifted into a moment of prophecy, a prophecy which I now offer to you:

The gift that God has placed inside of you is a beacon, a tracking device. The gift is summoned to the area of need. We think that we are moving from place to place, job to job, or church to church because of some human result or decision when in all actuality it is the gift that is being obedient to the Spirit that implanted it with in us.

The gift is the remote-control car, the drone for you new age folks, and God has the remote *control*. The scripture says that the gift will **make** room for you.

KNIT

The definition of make is to cause something to exist or come about. This means that our gifts create existence in places where existence did not exist. The gift makes room, it creates a space or void that only the gift can fill. Therefore, it brings you into positions before great men and women, because nothing else can fill the void that YOUR gift created, but YOU! If someone or something tried to fill the space it wouldn't fit because your gift created the room and your gift is the perfect fit!

The gift has no regard for you, your feelings or your level of comfort. The only thing the gift knows is that it has a demand and it is dedicated to supplying what is being demanded, YOU. The gift is somewhat of a bully. It will pick at you and pick on you. It will pick you out of a crowd of people who were more qualified, more charismatic, and more talented than you.

The gift will taunt you and keep you up at night. It will push you into places and platforms that you would have never agreed to on your own. The gift is demanding because it is demanded. The entire earth and all of its creation is stretching out its neck, watching and patiently awaiting your reveal. The gift is following the roar and groaning of the earth, because it is on assignment to liberate sinners and to be a witness to the deity (divine status, quality, or nature) of Jesus.

KNIT

As the gift develops and comes into its full-grown state it will outgrow mediocrity and small dreams. It will require new and bigger rooms. Rooms with more space to grow, flex and stretch. It begins a cycle of pushing and pulling causing all sorts of discomfort. We call this stretching and discomfort "wanting to do more" or "boredom".

I love this in Romans 8:22, "For we know that the whole creation groaneth and travaileth in pain together until NOW." Until NOW. There was a time when there was a waiting for a sign that the sons of God existed. But there is no longer a wait, the Spirit bears witness with our spirit that we are children of God.

The children of God, Kingdom sons and daughters of the Royal establishment sets the standard and showcase the proof a divinely orchestrated life. We bring the Word to life and to the lives of others. Our gift is one of the vehicles by which we accomplish this mission.

It is a shame that we are living to make a living yet never living. The systems of the earth have convinced most of us that we should strive to be cast into the leading role in the dream of a country, culture, or creed yet denying our mandate, calling, and election.

God gave us gifts in eternity for eternity. As He *knit* us together in utero, He included the ability to get wealth (Deuteronomy 8:18) by giving us what the

KNIT

earth needs and cannot live without. We have an insight as believers to the divine instruments needed to quiet the rumbling of malnourished purpose.

Maybe you are unsure of your gift. I encourage you to sit with the Creator, to be intentional about discovering who you were predestined to be in the earth. Speak to leaders who you can trust about developing you and your gift. Yes, there is a two-part development. Natural immaturity will serve to be a breach to spiritual development when its importance to be acknowledge is not taken seriously.

There must be an intercourse, an intimacy before there is a conception. The word intercourse means communication or dealings between individuals. The word conception means the forming or devising of a plan or idea, or genesis. God must speak to you and you must speak to God. The only way that a plan can be devised for your success that you can conceive and perceive is through the dealings between you and Him.

God, the Father, made the unconditional choice to give us the gift and the call without repentance (Romans 11:29). God knew that the gift would be perfect for you. He knew that your life, your story, and your journey would make good use of the gift. The gift He chose for you is something that you will use, and something you need. He put thought into the gift He gave you.

KNIT

The book of Matthew chapter seven verse eleven asks us this, "if you then, though you are evil, know how to give good gifts to your children, how much more will your Father in heaven give good gifts to those who ask him!"

He gives good gifts! Not the kind that you hope came with a gift receipt so you can take it back and get what you really wanted. Not only are they good gifts, but they are gifts that are in demand.

Your gift demands you to go further, to grow bigger to dare to be bolder than you could ever imagine. Your gift is busting the package at the seam. You are full of greatness and I give you permission to EXPLODE into purpose and be charged into destiny!

Father, I come into agreement with Your Holy Spirit. I will not stifle the Holy Spirit. I will not scoff at prophecies but will test everything that is said. Help me to hold on to what is good and stay away from every kind of evil. I desire to be meat for Your use Master and fulfill all that you have knit me to do in the earth. Gracious Father, please give me a greater sense of discernment for where my gifts are being demanded. Please give me the courage and wisdom to pursue destiny. Please remove every stitch of insecurity and feeling of inferiority. Thank you for choosing me. In Jesus name I pray. Amen.

KNIT

KNIT

-Reflect-

six

Let's Name It Grace

2 Timothy 1:9

For God saved us and called us to live a holy life. He did this, not because we deserved it, but because that was his plan from before the beginning of time--to show us his grace through Christ Jesus.

Guess what my Friend? God always knew that it would be impossible for you to do right. Sorry to break the news to you, but all have sinned, even you and me. That is why God had a plan to save us and call us to a holy life. You, all alone, are not able to accomplish living a holy life; therefore, the Father in all His wisdom gave us Jesus. No, you and I are not holy in our own right, but because Jesus was given as ransom for our sins, we are holy through Him.

The issue for most people is that we have not yet received this revelation in its entirety. We still get wrapped up in our flaws and our short comings; denying ourselves the right to be called, because of the knots of life. Do you think God is that fickle

KNIT

minded or naïve that He didn't consider all the things that would cause us to be entangled? I certainly hope not! It was always His plan to show us grace. Ephesians 1:7 ensures us that He is so rich in kindness and *grace* that he purchased our freedom with the blood of his Son and forgave our sins. We were *purchased* not *perfect.* We were never going to be in perfect condition for purchase, but God paid the costliest fee for you and me.

We are being perfected. God is perfecting the saints which can be translated that God is completing us. During the competing process we have been given the gift of grace. We have been given time and space to come into a right relationship with the Father; to understand the truth about His grace.

Just as God's grace changed our lives from the day we first heard of His grace and understood the truth about God's wonderful grace (Colossians 1:6); God's grace is an ongoing never-ending life changer. Grace will constantly and continuously change our lives as the completing process progresses in the direction of becoming like Jesus. God knit grace into the woven fabrics of our lives. Grace has the potency or the power to influence and make an impression for our success in the Kingdom, especially when fully understood *and* embraced.

Many Christ followers wrestle with "the sin factor." Let me attempt to help someone out. Grace does not give us permission to sin. When a believer sins there should be a process that happens initiated by conviction. Our love for Jesus and our gratitude for the sacrifice He made should cause us to desire to deny sin. Sin for a believer should put a greater weight on us not to sin.

Remember, it's about having a relationship, not about gaining a religion. In our relationship with Jesus we express love and gratitude. Our affections toward Jesus are strong therefore we denounce all things that are an enemy against Him. Grace abounds much more than sin (Romans 5:20). The grace of God gives us the ability and power to resist the things that war against our soul. For this reason, a believer who is ignorant to the truth about grace is a powerless believer.

I love the correlation between 2 Corinthians 12:9 and James 4:6. In 2 Corinthians 12:9 God says, "My grace is sufficient for you…" then in James we are reminded that God gives more grace. God has a sufficient (enough, plenty, adequate) supply of grace. He is generous and giving more grace to us. So why do we get in knots about our shortcomings? Why does it take us three weeks to snap out of guilt and condemnation? Why can't we accept both ends of God's grace and become better, wiser, stronger?

One end of grace says, "I have the power to live upright and not be a slave to sin." The other side of grace say, "When I do fail, I am forgiven." We

KNIT

should put both into practice. We should repent and receive God's forgiveness, but we should also know that we have the grace to resist temptation.

Let us therefore come boldly unto the throne of grace (unmerited favor) …that we may find grace (supernatural enablement and empowerment) to help in time of need (Hebrews 4:16). Understand this my dear Friend, not only does God want to give you favor and forgiveness, He also wants you to partake in the gift of empowerment. He empowers us to accomplish everything that we were knit to do while here on this earth.

God has given some the grace to be a business owner, some the grace to lead congregations, some the grace to understand medicine, etc. Grace strides together with purpose and destiny empowering us to live as Kingdom citizens in a land that is not our own. Grace gives you the ability to do things that is difficult for others to do. That's Gods favor!

Before you ever made a single mistake, God chose to love you. God knows your ignorance, and your limited knowledge base. He is even mindful of your moments of idiocy. He is the Master Mathematician. He calculated all of that and issued you a measure of faith.

For I say, through the *grace* given to me, to everyone who is among you, not to think of himself more highly than he ought to think, but to think

KNIT

soberly, as God has dealt to each one a measure of faith (Romans 12:3).

In other words, acknowledge that you have flaws and know that for that reason God gave you faith! It takes faith to have a proper perspective about yourself and about God. It takes faith in order to take both of those and use them to make the changes that need to be made in you. It takes faith to do right and to think right!

By faith we receive grace. Romans 8:26 tells us this truth, "And the Holy Spirit helps us in our weakness. For example, we don't know what God wants us to pray for. But the Holy Spirit prays for us with groanings that cannot be expressed in words." God is just that great. He gave us the Holy Spirit to help us understand grace. He knows that you and I need help. He knows that you and I will have moments of weakness requiring divine help.

God is not setting us up to fail. He has made every possible provision for us to succeed. If we continue reading Romans chapter 8, we will see in verse 27 that it says, "the Spirit pleads for us believers." That is how much God desires for us to be in fellowship with Him. So much that His very own Spirit works on our behalf to ensure that we are in right standing with God. It may seem hard to understand how it is possible for us to be forgiven and fought for. God pursues us in spite of ourselves and our inability to be absolutely perfect. Truth of the matter is that we

KNIT

are forgiven, and God is still relentlessly pursuing His people. It may seem crazy, but that my Friend is grace.

Father, it is You who I seek when my inner self is ashamed and cowardly. It is You who hear the words that I don't say and Who sees me when I'm hiding behind excuses and justifications. You, Father, are the God who sees me yet loves me in spite of what You see. Please mold my mind in such a way that I can become conscious of Your grace. Father, I desire to journey every corridor of the love that You have for me. Father, please help me to see me the way You see me and to grow according to the pace You've set for me. Let me never miss the promises that are locked up in the process. You are Adonai, my Redeemer. Amen.

KNIT

-Reflect-

Conclusion

Long before you and I were in utero God considered every breath we would take from our first breath until our last. He knows about every problem and every pain that we would encounter. God knows the decisions we will face and the amount of grace it would take to keep us encouraged to continue this race.

How powerful would it be if we sat back and let the story of our lives play out? What will happen if we stop fighting against God and come to the realization that He really does know what He is doing? How would life look for you if you decided to believe that God knows everything that you don't know?

Humans in our limited knowledge and understanding are accustomed to trying to figure things out. This behavior, in my opinion is one of our biggest issues. We are trying to figure out what has already been established. As unpopular as it may seem, seeking God for what's next is and will always be the formula for living this life on earth. He wrote the book therefore He has the answers.

The good news is, there is absolutely nothing that we will experience in this life that has snuck pass God! Things may get uncomfortable for us because we only know what we know. Most often it is not

KNIT

the situation that causes discomfort, it is the not knowing. We are often afraid of the unknown, the outcome, or how long we will be stuck in a situation. Each day that we live is a new day, a day that we have never lived before. A day full of unknowns. We learn how to navigate each day with the wisdom. We learned from the days before and the guidance that we receive from God, either through His word or through time spent in prayer.

No matter what the day may bring we can rest assure that we were knit for it. We were strategically placed. I would like to go back to Isaiah 55:8-9 where the Lord declares, "My thoughts are not your thoughts, neither are your ways My ways." I'm reminded of several instances in the Word where God's ways did not make sense to man.

One story that sticks out to me is the story of Hosea. I do not think it is a coincidence that in the book where God instructs His prophet to marry a prostitute, He also says that His people are destroyed for lack of knowledge. The New Living Translation says, "My people are being destroyed because they don't know Me." Where we fail often is believing that we have God figured out. We consider what seems right in our sight and we proceed in life based off of our assumptions of what is right and wrong.

KNIT

If you and I were to be real, we would agree that if our son or nephew told us that God told him to marry a prostitute, we would not believe that he heard from God. But God indeed gave this instruction to Hosea. My point is this, just because it doesn't fit into our perfect array of situations and solutions doesn't mean that God did not purpose it in our lives. God gave Hosea instruction to send a message to His people. Why did God allow the out of the ordinary to happen in your life? Was it ever about you? Or was it to demonstrate His very own power?

God tells His story and communicates His plans through our lives and all His creation. Recall the use of animals in the scriptures, and the use of trees. God is telling us what He is made of and the position of His heart. There is no way that we can truly grip all the ways He moves the world forward towards His ultimate plan, which by the way, you and I are a part of. You and me, our good days and bad days, our drama, our bad decisions, our quirky ways, and our weird ideas. He has the capacity to use it ALL to move the world in His direction.

My prayer for you and all mankind is that we become "ok" with the plan that God has already made. I believe that stress levels will decrease, real joy will burst forth, and life will be lived to the fullest once we understand that He is a good Father, a Wonderful Counselor, and the Wisest most

KNIT

Loving Leader that a man or woman could ever have.

His plans are to give us a hope and a future. He will not ruin His reputation therefore victory must be our portion. He will get the glory and be glorified in our lives and for this very reason we will always win! Even in death we win because we are elevated to heavenly places, the ultimate promotion.

Life and society will temp us to believe that God is limited and reactive. He is neither. In our limits we must be careful not to limit God. We do not know all the possible solutions to a problem, only God does, and the solutions are limitless. He does not wait for you and me to screw up or lose our crap before He decides what we are worthy of. He decided that we were worthy when He allow Jesus to be beaten, battered, bruised, and murdered.

What Jesus had to suffer does not make sense. What you have suffered may not make sense, but God is going to cause you to triumph and you will rise up with power. You will be a champion for others as Jesus is a Champion for us!

Imagine the pattern of your life, one needle, one string. God as the knitter, you as the needle, life as the string. As God is holding you, guiding you, the string follows. The string may get knotted, but the needle is always safe in Gods hand. And sometimes God must take the needle back through to untie the knot because the knot is not a part of the design. No

KNIT

matter the twists and turns of the string, God is faithful to complete the work He has already begun therefore you can look over your life and say, "I was *knit* for this!"

Father, I repent. I often forget that You know me better than I know myself. Who am I that You would be mindful of me? Please help me to forever remember that You have been and always will be in total control. My mind cannot always comprehend the truth that You foreknew me. When I feel like life is weaving a trap remind me that You hold the needle and You will never let go. Help me to have the right perspective about You, Your plan, and the value You have placed in me. Write Your truth on my heart, engrain it in every fiber of my being. May I never prick You with my resistance to Your plan. I love You and desire to learn to love You even more. In Jesus name I pray. Amen.

KNIT

-Reflect-

Made in the USA
Las Vegas, NV
04 May 2023